Insect World
Cicadas

by Mari Schuh

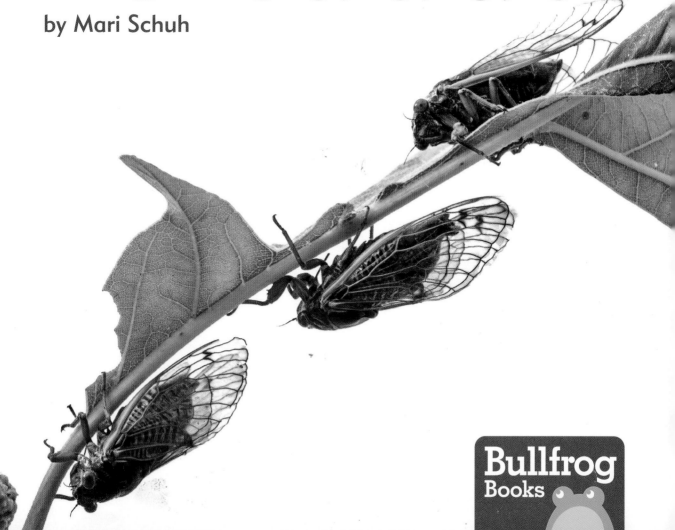

Bullfrog Books

Ideas for Parents and Teachers

Bullfrog Books let children practice reading informational text at the earliest reading levels. Repetition, familiar words, and photo labels support early readers.

Before Reading

• Discuss the cover photo. What does it tell them?

• Look at the picture glossary together. Read and discuss the words.

Read the Book

• "Walk" through the book and look at the photos. Let the child ask questions. Point out the photo labels.

• Read the book to the child, or have him or her read independently.

After Reading

• Prompt the child to think more. Ask: Have you ever seen a cicada? Where was it? Have you heard them buzzing?

Bullfrog Books are published by Jump!
5357 Penn Avenue South
Minneapolis, MN 55419
www.jumplibrary.com

Library of Congress Cataloging-in-Publication Data

Schuh, Mari C., 1975– author.
  Cicadas / by Mari Schuh.
     pages cm. — (Insect world)
  Summary: "This photo-illustrated book for early readers tells about the life cycle of cicadas. Includes picture glossary" — Provided by publisher.
  Audience: Ages 5-8.
  Audience: K to grade 3.
  Includes index.
  ISBN 978-1-62031-160-8 (hardcover) —
  ISBN 978-1-62496-247-9 (ebook)
  1. Cicadas — Juvenile literature. I. Title.
QL527.C5S38 2015
595.7'52 — dc23
                                    2014025458

Series Editor: Rebecca Glaser
Series Designer: Ellen Huber
Book Designer: Anna Peterson
Photo Researcher: Casie Cook

Photo Credits: All photos by Shutterstock except: Alamy, 13, 14–15; Alexander Wild, 1, 5, 20–21; Fiona Dudley, 10–11; National Geographic Creative, 16–17; SuperStock, 6–7, 23tl; Thinkstock, 4, 8–9, 19, 23bl, 23br.

Printed in the United States of America at Corporate Graphics, in North Mankato, Minnesota.

Table of Contents

Loud Bugs

A cicada sings in a tree.
Buzz. Buzz.

Oh, wow!

He is so loud.

He sings to find a female.

Can she hear him?

female

Yes. Here she is!

They mate.

She makes
holes in twigs.

Why?

She lays her
eggs there.

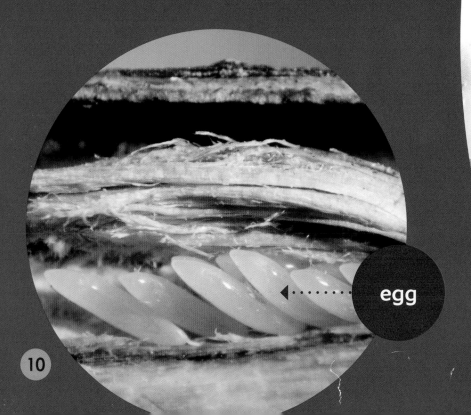

egg

They drop to the ground.

The nymphs dig.

They live underground.

Some live there
for a long time.

How long?

For 17 years!

The nymphs grow
and grow.

They shed their
old skin.

Now they are ready
for a new home.

They dig out
of the soil.

Here is a tree to climb.
Up they go!

They shed their skin again.

Now they are all grown up.

Buzz! Buzz!

Parts of a Cicada

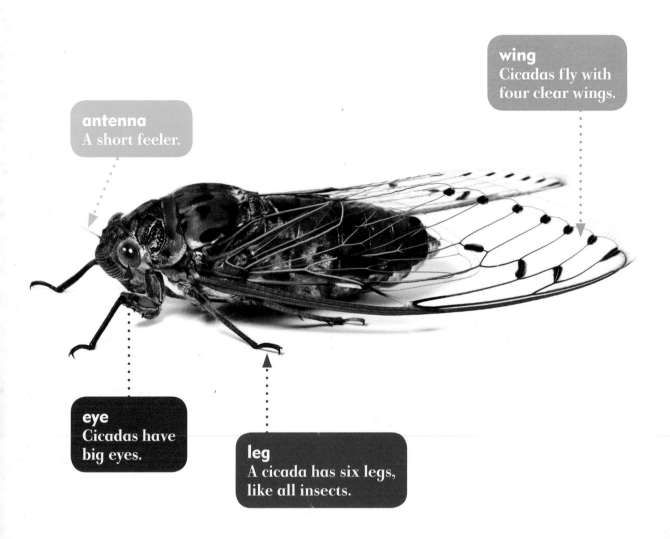

antenna
A short feeler.

wing
Cicadas fly with four clear wings.

eye
Cicadas have big eyes.

leg
A cicada has six legs, like all insects.

Picture Glossary

female
An animal that can give birth or lay eggs.

nymph
A young cicada.

mate
To join together to make young.

shed
To fall off or get rid of; nymphs shed their skin many times as they grow.

Index

To Learn More

Learning more is as easy as 1, 2, 3.

1) Go to www.factsurfer.com

2) Enter "cicadas" into the search box.

3) Click the "Surf" button to see a list of websites.

With factsurfer.com, finding more information is just a click away.